THE ULTIMATE FAN
SABRI
CARPENTER

CH00970751

LIFE STORY, FUN FACTS, QUIZZES, JOURNALING PROMPTS AND MORE

Table of Contents

Where It All Begins.................................. 1

The First Notes...................................... 11

Crafting a Signature Sound................... 22

The Breakthrough Moment................... 32

The Rise to Stardom............................. 42

Inspiring Collaborations........................ 51

Overcoming Obstacles.......................... 59

Celebrating Achievements..................... 69

Fashion, Favorites, and Fan Bonds........ 77

Fun Reflections..................................... 88

introduction

Welcome, dear readers! I invite you to embark on a delightful journey through the enchanting world of Sabrina Carpenter. This book is crafted with love and care, much like a cozy story shared between a grandmother and her little ones. Inside these pages, you'll discover the incredible life story of Sabrina, a young star whose talent shines as brightly as the sun.

From her early days, filled with dreams and melodies, to her rise as a beloved artist, Sabrina's journey is a tapestry woven with joy, hard work, and resilience. You'll learn about the milestones that have shaped her career, the challenges she's faced, and the beautiful collaborations that have enriched her artistic path.

But that's not all! This book is bursting with fun facts that will tickle your fancy, quizzes that will challenge your knowledge, and heartwarming journaling prompts to inspire you to reflect on your own dreams and experiences. Each chapter is designed to be both entertaining and enriching, perfect for fans of all ages. Whether you're a lifelong follower or just beginning to explore her music and magic, there's something here for everyone.

So, snuggle up with a warm blanket and a cup of cocoa, and let's dive into the wonderful world of Sabrina Carpenter together! There's wisdom to be found, laughter to be shared, and memories to be made as we celebrate the life of this extraordinary artist.

Chapter 1

- A Glimpse into Childhood: Explore Sabrina's early years and family life, including her upbringing and formative experiences.
- The Spark of Passion: Discover the moments that ignited her love for music, from singing in the shower to performing for friends and family.
- Early Influences: Learn about the artists and experiences that inspired her creative journey, from Disney movies to family traditions.

Where It All Begins

A Glimpse into Childhood

Once upon a time, in the charming little town of Lehigh Valley, Pennsylvania, a bright star began to shine. Her name was Sabrina Carpenter, a lovely girl born on May 11, 1999. From a young age, she had a sparkle in her eyes and a song in her heart. Sabrina was the youngest of three sisters, raised in a warm and loving household, where music flowed as freely as laughter.

Sabrina's parents, Elizabeth and David Carpenter, played a vital role in nurturing her creative spirit. Elizabeth, a former singer and vocal coach, had an immense influence on Sabrina's love for music. Her dad, David, worked as a construction worker and made sure that the family was always comfortable, creating a home filled with support and encouragement. Sabrina often recalls how her mom would sing around the house, turning everyday moments into a joyous melody.

Growing up, Sabrina was surrounded by the love of her family. She had two older sisters, Sarah and Shannon, who would often play dress-up and encourage her imaginative play. The Carpenter home was a place where creativity flourished. Sabrina loved to put on shows for her family, performing songs she'd learned from her mother or choreographing little dances in the living room.

As a child, Sabrina was a curious little one, always eager to explore the world around her. She had a fondness for the outdoors, often playing with her friends in the neighborhood. One of her favorite pastimes was climbing trees, where she could daydream about becoming a famous singer. She loved animals too, especially her dog, who was her constant companion during adventures. Sabrina would often express her love for animals in her early drawings, showcasing her artistic talents even back then.

Sabrina's family would take regular trips to nearby places like the Pocono Mountains, where they enjoyed nature hikes and cozy campfires under the stars. These moments instilled in her a deep appreciation for family and the beauty of the world around her. It was during one of these family outings that she discovered her love for storytelling, weaving tales of magic and wonder for her sisters.

When Sabrina was just seven years old, her family decided to move to Los Angeles, California, in search of new opportunities. This move was a significant change, but it also opened doors to Sabrina's dreams.

She immersed herself in the vibrant culture of the city, soaking up everything it had to offer. The bright lights and bustling energy of Los Angeles inspired her even more to pursue her passion for performing.

At school, Sabrina quickly became known for her talent. She participated in school plays and talent shows, captivating her classmates with her singing and acting skills. One of her earliest performances was in a school production of "The Wizard of Oz," where she played Dorothy. It was a magical moment that solidified her desire to be on stage.

While juggling her academics and blossoming career, Sabrina also had some favorite childhood treats. She adored chocolate chip cookies, which her mom often baked on weekends, filling their home with a delightful aroma. On special occasions, she would ask for her favorite dish, macaroni and cheese, a simple but comforting meal that reminded her of home.

As her passion for music grew, Sabrina began taking acting lessons, which allowed her to hone her skills further. She made her television debut in 2012 on the Disney Channel show "Girl Meets World," a spin-off of the beloved series "Boy Meets World."

This role was a turning point in her life, leading her to achieve her dreams and inspiring countless fans along the way.

In those early years, Sabrina Carpenter was not just a girl with dreams; she was a shining example of how family love, creativity, and a sprinkle of magic can pave the way for greatness. As she navigated the ups and downs of childhood, she learned the importance of resilience and staying true to herself. Little did she know, this was only the beginning of her extraordinary journey in the world of music and entertainment.

The Spark of Passion

As young Sabrina Carpenter blossomed into a spirited girl, her passion for music began to flicker like a candle in a gentle breeze. It was in the cozy corners of her childhood home that she first found her voice—whether it was in the shower, where she belted out songs with glee, or in the living room, where she transformed into a mini superstar for her family and friends.

One of Sabrina's earliest memories was singing along to the enchanting melodies of her favorite Disney songs. Her mom, Elizabeth, would often hum tunes from The Little Mermaid or Beauty and the Beast, and Sabrina would mimic every note, her voice echoing through the halls. She adored the way music made her feel—a magical escape from the ordinary, filling her with joy and excitement.

At school, she was known for her lively spirit and infectious laughter. Her friends, like Kayla and Emily, became her biggest cheerleaders, encouraging her to perform at birthday parties and school events. Together, they would create dance routines and put on impromptu shows in their backyards, filled with giggles and dreams of stardom.

. Sabrina loved to sing Taylor Swift and Katy Perry songs, and her friends would often join in, creating a chorus of youthful joy.

One special moment stands out vividly in her memory. It was her eighth birthday party, and her parents surprised her with a karaoke machine. Oh, what a delight it was! Sabrina and her friends spent hours singing their hearts out, taking turns to showcase their talents. As she sang "Firework" by Katy Perry, Sabrina felt a thrill she had never known before. Her heart swelled with happiness, knowing she was born to perform.

Beyond the joyful gatherings, Sabrina often found solace in music while watching her mother practice. Elizabeth would sit at the piano, her fingers dancing over the keys, filling the room with melodies. Sabrina would sit beside her, mesmerized, dreaming of the day she would create such beautiful music herself. Those moments were seeds of inspiration, nurturing her love for singing and songwriting.

Early Influences

Every great artist is shaped by the world around them, and for young Sabrina Carpenter, her early influences were as colorful as a painter's palette. Growing up in a loving household in Lehigh Valley, Pennsylvania, Sabrina was surrounded by a blend of music, storytelling, and creativity that sparked her imagination from an early age.

One of the most significant influences in her life came from the enchanting world of animated films. Like many children, Sabrina adored the magical tales that graced the screen, but for her, they were more than just movies; they were gateways to her dreams. She would spend countless hours captivated by the enchanting songs that brought the characters to life. With her sparkling blue eyes wide with wonder, she would sing along, imagining herself as a star on the big screen.

Her favorite scene involved a curious girl longing to discover the world beyond her home, and she loved to recreate these moments with her sister, Sarah. They would turn their living room into a magical kingdom, complete with makeshift costumes crafted from sheets and towels. The sisters would perform for their parents, David and Elizabeth, who encouraged their imaginative play and cherished the infectious laughter that filled their home.

But it wasn't just animated films that inspired Sabrina. Her family also played a crucial role in shaping her creative spirit. She grew up in a household rich in musical traditions, where her mother would often play the guitar and her father would sing folk songs around the campfire during summer evenings. David, a skilled musician himself, would strum melodies that brought the family together. This musical foundation provided Sabrina with a deep appreciation for storytelling through song, and she often found herself humming along, caught up in the magic of the moment.

Additionally, the vibrant community around her offered a treasure trove of inspiration. Local talent shows and school performances became platforms for Sabrina to watch and learn from others. She was particularly drawn to the older girls in her neighborhood, who sang in the school choir and participated in theatrical productions. Their confidence and passion ignited a fire within her. One summer, she attended a local musical theater camp where she was introduced to a wider range of music and performance styles. There, she met a mentor, Miss Linda, who recognized Sabrina's potential and encouraged her to embrace her unique voice.

Family traditions also left a lasting impact on her journey. Every winter, the Carpenter family would gather for a cozy holiday celebration where they would sing carols and share stories. This annual ritual fostered a sense of belonging and encouraged Sabrina to explore her creativity. Those moments around the fireplace, with hot cocoa in hand and laughter echoing through the room, instilled a sense of warmth that Sabrina carried into her music.

Through the melodies of beloved songs, the folk tunes of her father, and the vibrant performances of her community, Sabrina Carpenter was molded into the artist she would soon become. Each note and every story was a stepping stone, leading her to the realization that music was not just a hobby; it was her calling.

Chapter 2

- Writing Her First Songs: Dive into the creativity behind Sabrina's earliest compositions and the themes that inspired them.
- Performing for the First Time: Relive the excitement and nerves of her initial performances, including school events and local showcases.
- Sharing the Joy: Understand how sharing music became a source of happiness for her and how she connected with audiences.

The First Notes

Writing Her First Songs

As Sabrina Carpenter navigated the waters of her early musical journey, she began to dip her toes into the art of songwriting. At just nine years old, she discovered the exhilarating world of creating her own melodies. The spark ignited when she received her first guitar for her birthday, a beautiful instrument gifted by her father, David. With its glossy wood finish and sweet sound, the guitar quickly became her cherished companion.

Sabrina spent countless afternoons strumming away, experimenting with different chords and sounds. The gentle strumming of her guitar became a soundtrack for her budding imagination. During this time, she drew inspiration from the stories around her—the people she loved, the dreams she held, and the everyday moments that painted her life. In her little notebook, filled with pink and purple doodles, she began jotting down lyrics that reflected her thoughts and feelings.

One of her first songs, penned around the age of ten, was a heartfelt piece about friendship, inspired by her bond with her childhood friend, Gigi. The lyrics captured the essence of their adventures, from bike rides through the neighborhood to their late-night talks under the stars.

Each word was infused with the joy of companionship, and her innocence shone through in every line. The simple, catchy chorus reflected her youthful spirit:

"Together we'll chase the sun, laughing 'til the day is done."

Sabrina also drew influence from the experiences of her family. Her older sister, Sarah, was a constant source of support and inspiration, encouraging Sabrina to express herself through music. When Sarah faced challenges in school, Sabrina penned a song titled "Keep Your Head Up," which served as a motivational anthem to remind her sister to persevere. This song showcased Sabrina's early understanding of the power of music to heal and uplift others.

In addition to personal experiences, her creative mind was influenced by the vibrant world around her. She would often write about the natural beauty of her hometown, inspired by the lush greenery of Pennsylvania. On long walks with her mother, Elizabeth, she would absorb the sights and sounds of their surroundings. It was during one such walk, surrounded by blooming wildflowers and the soft whisper of the wind, that she penned a song about nature titled "Whispers in the Breeze."

The lyrics celebrated the magic of the world, capturing moments of tranquility and wonder.

Sabrina's songwriting process was often playful and spontaneous. She'd gather her friends, including Gigi and their mutual friend, Kaitlyn, to sing and brainstorm ideas. They would spend afternoons in Sabrina's backyard, creating melodies that echoed through the neighborhood. The laughter and camaraderie of those sessions became the foundation for Sabrina's artistic voice.

By the age of eleven, she had a small collection of original songs, each a reflection of her growth and development as an artist. While she may not have realized it then, these early compositions were laying the groundwork for her future success. Her songwriting was a beautiful tapestry woven from her experiences, her friendships, and the magic of her imagination.

With each new song, Sabrina was not just creating music; she was crafting her identity as an artist, ready to share her heart with the world. This journey of creativity and self-expression would soon lead her to new stages and larger audiences, setting the stage for her remarkable rise in the music industry.

Performing for the First Time

As the sun shone brightly on a beautiful spring day, Sabrina Carpenter's heart raced with excitement and nerves. She was about to step onto the stage for her very first public performance, a milestone that would forever mark her journey as an artist. The setting was her elementary school's talent show, a cherished event where students showcased their talents to friends, family, and teachers.

At just eleven years old, Sabrina felt a mix of exhilaration and trepidation. With her guitar slung over her shoulder, she stood backstage, peeking through the curtains to see the audience—smiling faces of classmates and proud parents. Among them were her family members, including her mother, Elizabeth, who had always encouraged her to pursue her passions. Elizabeth beamed with pride, whispering words of encouragement, assuring Sabrina that it was just a chance to share her love for music.

When it was finally her turn, Sabrina took a deep breath and stepped onto the stage. The lights were bright, but they illuminated her path to confidence. As she settled onto the small wooden stool, she looked out at the crowd, and her nerves began to settle.

She started strumming her guitar, feeling the familiar comfort of the instrument beneath her fingers. She decided to perform one of her original songs, "Keep Your Head Up," a piece she had written for her sister, Sarah.

As the first notes filled the air, Sabrina felt an undeniable connection with the audience. The initial anxiety faded away, replaced by a sense of joy and empowerment. She poured her heart into each lyric, her voice resonating with sincerity. The energy in the room shifted; laughter, clapping, and supportive cheers followed each verse. Her classmates sang along, harmonizing the catchy chorus that encouraged perseverance.

Sabrina's performance not only showcased her talent but also revealed the importance of community support in her life. Friends like Gigi and Kaitlyn, who were in the audience, cheered her on, their faces glowing with excitement. After the performance, they rushed to congratulate her, enveloping her in hugs and smiles, reinforcing the bond they shared through music.

That night, as Sabrina sat with her family at dinner, her heart swelled with happiness.

She couldn't stop talking about how much she loved performing, recounting every detail of her experience, from the rush of adrenaline to the way the audience responded. Her parents praised her courage, and Elizabeth shared stories of her own experiences on stage, encouraging Sabrina to continue pursuing her dreams.

As she lay in bed that night, Sabrina reflected on how music had transformed her. It wasn't just about singing and playing; it was a way to connect with others, express herself, and find joy. That first performance ignited a fire within her, paving the way for future endeavors in music. From that day on, Sabrina embraced every opportunity to perform, knowing that she had the power to touch hearts and inspire others through her songs.

Little did she know, this moment was just the beginning. As she continued to hone her craft, she would step onto much larger stages, sharing her voice with countless fans around the world. The excitement of her first performance would forever remain a cherished memory, reminding her of the magic that happens when you follow your heart and share your passion.

Sharing the Joy

As Sabrina Carpenter blossomed into her teenage years, the joy of sharing her music became an essential part of her life. It was more than just a hobby; it was a way to connect with others and spread happiness. Through her heartfelt lyrics and melodies, she created a bridge between herself and her audience, fostering a deep sense of community.

At local coffee shops and community events, Sabrina eagerly took the stage, sharing her latest compositions with anyone who would listen. With her guitar in hand and her warm smile lighting up the room, she poured her heart into each performance. Friends, family, and even new fans would gather, eager to experience the magic of her music. Among them were her childhood friends, Gigi and Kaitlyn, who became her biggest supporters, cheering her on from the front row.

One of Sabrina's favorite moments was participating in open mic nights at a quaint little café called The Coffee House, located in her hometown of Valencia, California. The intimate atmosphere provided a safe space for artists and aspiring musicians to share their talents. Every Tuesday night, she would eagerly sign up, waiting for her turn to perform.

As she listened to others share their stories through song, she felt inspired and understood, realizing that they all shared a common love for music.

During these performances, Sabrina's songs began to resonate with her audience in ways she never expected. One evening, she performed an original piece titled "All We Have Is Love," a heartfelt anthem about friendship and connection. As she sang, she noticed several audience members swaying gently, lost in the music, some even wiping away tears. It was in that moment she truly understood the power of her gift—the ability to uplift others through her art.

Sharing her music also meant sharing her life experiences, and Sabrina found herself connecting with her fans on a personal level. After each performance, she would take the time to chat with those who approached her, often learning their stories and struggles. Many shared how her songs inspired them during tough times, bringing them comfort and hope. This mutual exchange of joy was heartwarming; she could see how her music made a difference in their lives, just as it did in hers.

In the summers, she participated in local music festivals, where her performances attracted larger crowds. The thrill of seeing people sing along to her songs was indescribable. At one festival, she introduced a song called "Eyes Wide Open," a reminder to embrace life's possibilities. As the audience sang the chorus in unison, Sabrina's heart swelled with pride. It felt like they were all part of something bigger, a shared celebration of life and creativity.

Sabrina's passion for sharing music extended beyond the stage. She also used social media to connect with fans, often posting videos of her singing in her bedroom, just as she did when she first started. These intimate glimpses into her life helped her followers feel closer to her, building a loyal community that cherished every note and lyric.

As her musical journey continued, Sabrina understood that sharing her songs was about more than entertainment; it was about creating connections, spreading joy, and inspiring others. With every performance, she embraced the magic of music, knowing that her voice had the power to make a lasting impact.

Each smile from the audience, every heartfelt conversation after a show, and all the shared laughter became a testament to the joy that music brings to life. It was clear to her: the love of sharing music was a beautiful gift, one she would cherish forever.

Chapter 3

- Finding Her Voice: Explore how Sabrina developed her unique vocal style and her journey through vocal training.
- Genres and Influences: Discover the musical genres that shaped her sound, from pop to folk, and the artists she admired.
- Creating Memorable Melodies: Learn about the songwriting process and techniques she uses, including co-writing with other musicians.

Crafting a Signature Sound

Finding Her Voice

Sabrina Carpenter's journey to finding her unique vocal style was as colorful and layered as her personality. From a young age, she was surrounded by music, but it wasn't until her early teenage years that she began to consciously shape her sound. Growing up in a musical household, she often listened to a wide range of genres. Her parents, David and Elizabeth, nurtured her love for music, exposing her to everything from classic rock to contemporary pop.

When Sabrina was around 12 years old, she took the brave step of enrolling in vocal lessons to refine her singing technique. This decision marked a significant turning point in her life. Under the guidance of vocal coach, Rachel Stoll, she began to explore her voice's full potential. Rachel, known for her supportive approach, helped Sabrina develop her range and breath control, instilling in her the importance of vocal health.

Sabrina learned various techniques, from proper warm-ups to breathing exercises, which helped her gain confidence. She recalls practicing scales in front of her bedroom mirror, imagining herself on stage, performing for fans. Rachel introduced her to various singing styles, allowing Sabrina to experiment with everything from jazz to pop.

Each lesson ignited her passion, revealing the unique tones she could produce.

It was during this time that Sabrina also discovered her natural affinity for storytelling through song. She learned that her voice could convey emotions, allowing her to connect with listeners on a deeper level. She often spent hours crafting songs that reflected her experiences, desires, and dreams. The process of vocal training taught her to express her individuality, making her voice an extension of who she was.

As she honed her skills, Sabrina participated in school talent shows and community performances, where she could showcase her progress. Each performance helped her build confidence, but it was during one pivotal event at the local theater that she truly found her voice. At the age of 13, she auditioned for a lead role in a musical adaptation of a beloved story. The experience was both exhilarating and nerve-wracking, but when she sang her audition piece, she felt an unmistakable sense of belonging.

After that performance, she received accolades from both her peers and audience members, including her supportive family, who cheered her on with pride.

This moment solidified her belief that music was not just a pastime but her true calling. It became clear to her that her voice had the power to resonate with others, and she cherished that connection.

As she continued her vocal journey, Sabrina attended summer workshops and music camps, meeting other aspiring artists and learning from experienced mentors. One notable workshop was the National Association of Teachers of Singing (NATS) conference, where she connected with vocalists from across the country. During this time, she formed friendships with fellow young artists, some of whom would later become collaborators.

Through dedication and hard work, Sabrina's voice began to evolve into a distinctive sound characterized by its warmth and authenticity. She learned to embrace her natural tone, understanding that her unique qualities were what made her special. It was important for her to remain true to herself while navigating the complexities of the music industry.

By the time she entered her teenage years, Sabrina had cultivated a vocal style that was unmistakably her own—a blend of youthful energy and mature emotion.

Genres and Influences

As a young girl, she listened to artists like Taylor Swift, whose storytelling ability and emotional depth resonated with her. Sabrina admired how Taylor's lyrics captured relatable experiences, and this inspired her own songwriting journey. Sabrina also found inspiration in the powerful vocals of artists like Adele and the playful pop sounds of Carly Rae Jepsen. The energy of these singers fueled her desire to create music that would touch hearts and bring joy to listeners.

While pop music was a significant influence, Sabrina's taste was not confined to one genre. She developed a fondness for folk sounds, appreciating the acoustic elements and storytelling aspects. This love for folk music was further nurtured by artists like Ed Sheeran, whose heartfelt lyrics and melodic charm inspired Sabrina to experiment with her songwriting. She often found herself captivated by the way these musicians combined personal experiences with universal themes, creating songs that resonated with audiences worldwide.

Sabrina's exploration of genres did not stop at pop and folk. She also delved into the world of R&B and jazz, appreciating their smooth melodies and intricate rhythms.

This exploration opened her ears to a new palette of sounds, and she began to incorporate these influences into her own music. As she matured as an artist, she embraced the idea of blending different genres, reflecting her eclectic taste.

During her teenage years, Sabrina attended concerts and music festivals, where she witnessed the magic of live performances. She admired artists like Hozier and Norah Jones, who captivated crowds with their soulful voices and compelling stage presence. Watching them perform solidified her ambition to connect with audiences on a similar level. Inspired by their charisma, Sabrina practiced her stage presence, learning to engage with listeners and create memorable moments.

In addition to her musical influences, Sabrina was deeply inspired by her family's musical traditions. Her parents, David and Elizabeth, often played music around the house, creating an environment that celebrated creativity. Sabrina's mother would sing lullabies and play folk songs on her guitar, while her father shared his love for classic rock. These family traditions instilled a sense of appreciation for music in Sabrina, fostering her desire to contribute to this beautiful art form.

As she honed her craft, Sabrina found herself collaborating with other musicians, further expanding her horizons. These partnerships allowed her to experiment with different sounds and styles, broadening her musical palette. She would often attend songwriting sessions with fellow artists, where they shared ideas and crafted melodies together. This collaborative spirit fueled her creativity, leading to the development of a sound that was uniquely hers.

By the time Sabrina stepped into the recording studio, she had a rich understanding of the genres that influenced her. She blended elements of pop, folk, and R&B, creating a sound that resonated with her personal experiences and artistic vision. Each song she crafted became a reflection of her journey, embodying the various influences that shaped her identity as an artist.

In her quest to find her signature sound, Sabrina learned that the key to authenticity was embracing her diverse influences while remaining true to herself. Her ability to blend genres and convey heartfelt emotions through her music allowed her to connect with listeners of all ages, making her a beloved figure in the industry.

Creating Memorable Melodies

As Sabrina Carpenter progressed in her musical journey, she discovered that the heart of her artistry lay in her ability to create memorable melodies that resonate with her audience. From the moment she picked up her first guitar at the age of 10, she began experimenting with different sounds and structures, seeking to craft tunes that would linger in listeners' minds long after the music stopped.

Sabrina's songwriting process is both intuitive and meticulous. She often begins by jotting down her thoughts and feelings in a journal, capturing the essence of her experiences. This practice allows her to explore themes that matter to her, whether it's the thrill of young love, the challenges of growing up, or the joy of friendship. By translating her emotions into words, she sets the foundation for her songs, creating a narrative that speaks to the hearts of her fans.

When it comes to crafting melodies, Sabrina draws inspiration from her favorite artists while also experimenting with her own voice. She often hums a tune or plays a few chords on her guitar, letting the music flow naturally.

This organic approach allows her to tap into her creativity without overthinking it. For instance, her song "Thumbs" showcases her ability to blend catchy hooks with relatable lyrics, a testament to her knack for melody-making.

Collaboration has also played a significant role in her songwriting journey. Working with other musicians has opened new doors for her creativity. Sabrina has teamed up with talented songwriters and producers, such as Evan "Kidd" Bogart and T. M. "Teddy" Lane, who have helped refine her sound and enhance her songwriting skills. Through these collaborations, she learned the importance of bouncing ideas off one another, leading to the creation of songs that combine their unique perspectives.

One of the standout aspects of Sabrina's songwriting is her ability to craft catchy choruses that encourage listeners to sing along. Her knack for creating earworms can be traced back to her early exposure to various musical genres. Sabrina believes that a great melody should evoke emotion and be relatable to a wide audience, allowing everyone to connect with her music. Songs like "All We Have Is Love" and "Skinny Dipping" exemplify this quality, as they feature infectious melodies that stay with listeners long after the song ends.

Additionally, Sabrina often draws from her own life experiences when writing. For instance, the song "In My Bed" was inspired by her personal journey of self-discovery and empowerment. By infusing her songs with authenticity, she ensures that her music reflects the ups and downs of her life, making it more relatable to her audience.

Another essential aspect of her songwriting process is the emphasis on storytelling. Sabrina knows that every song is an opportunity to share a piece of her heart, and she strives to convey genuine emotions through her lyrics. In her track "Skinny Dipping," she invites listeners into a world of carefree summer nights, encapsulating the joy of friendship and the thrill of new experiences. This ability to weave stories into her melodies makes her songs feel personal and inviting, drawing listeners in as if they're sharing an intimate moment with a close friend.

Sabrina's commitment to crafting memorable melodies has earned her a loyal fanbase that resonates with her music. Each song she creates is a reflection of her journey, allowing her to connect deeply with her audience.

Chapter 4

- The Key Performance: Uncover the pivotal performance that changed everything, including her breakthrough role in a notable project.
- Breaking into the Spotlight: Discover how she gained recognition in the music industry through a combination of talent and timing.
- The Impact of Social Media: Learn how platforms like YouTube and Instagram helped launch her career and connect with fans.

The Breakthrough Moment

The Key Performance

Every artist has a defining moment that propels them into the limelight, and for Sabrina Carpenter, that moment came during a performance that would change the course of her career forever. It was the summer of 2014 when Sabrina, then just 14 years old, auditioned for the Disney Channel series Girl Meets World, a spinoff of the beloved show Boy Meets World. Her audition showcased not only her acting prowess but also her burgeoning musical talent, as she performed an original song that she had written.

Sabrina's audition captivated the producers, who recognized her unique blend of charm and creativity. The role of Maya Hart was a perfect fit for her, and soon after, she was cast alongside an incredible ensemble, including Rowan Blanchard, who played her best friend, Riley. The series premiered on June 27, 2014, and from that moment on, Sabrina became a household name. Her portrayal of Maya resonated with audiences, who connected with the character's struggles and triumphs during the tumultuous teenage years.

The show's popularity provided a platform for Sabrina to showcase her musical talents. As she sang her heart out in various episodes, fans began to take notice of her impressive vocal skills. One notable moment was when she performed "Take on the World," a duet with Rowan that highlighted their characters' friendship and dreams. This performance struck a chord with viewers and demonstrated Sabrina's potential as both an actress and a singer.

In the same year, Sabrina made her debut on the Billboard charts with her single "Can't Blame a Girl for Trying." The song was released on March 11, 2014, and it perfectly captured the essence of her character in Girl Meets World. The track resonated with many young listeners, who saw themselves in Sabrina's lyrics about chasing dreams and navigating the ups and downs of adolescence. The music video showcased her infectious energy and natural charisma, and it quickly racked up millions of views on YouTube.

The pivotal performance during her audition, coupled with her role on Girl Meets World, set the stage for Sabrina's breakthrough in the entertainment industry.

It wasn't just a moment in the spotlight; it was the launchpad for a multifaceted career that would see her flourish as both an actress and a musician. As she began to tour and promote her music, audiences were drawn to her relatable lyrics and catchy melodies, solidifying her place in the hearts of fans.

Sabrina's journey from a bright-eyed teen to a rising star was a testament to her hard work and dedication. With each performance, she left audiences eager for more, creating a loyal fanbase that admired her authenticity and passion. This breakthrough moment not only opened doors for Sabrina but also marked the beginning of a remarkable journey that would take her across stages and screens, captivating hearts worldwide.

As she continued to grow, Sabrina embraced the responsibility that came with her newfound fame. She aimed to inspire others, especially young girls, to pursue their dreams fearlessly, just as she had done. With every song, every role, and every performance, she reminded her audience that magic happens when passion meets opportunity— and her journey was only just beginning.

Breaking into the Spotlight

After her memorable role in Girl Meets World, Sabrina Carpenter quickly transitioned from a promising young actress to a rising star in the music industry. Her first single, "Can't Blame a Girl for Trying," released in March 2014, not only showcased her vocal talent but also solidified her presence as a musician. The song climbed the charts, making waves on Billboard's Heatseekers chart and earning her recognition as an artist in her own right. The catchy lyrics and relatable themes captured the hearts of many, especially her young fans who found comfort in her message of self-acceptance and perseverance.

As Sabrina navigated her newfound fame, she understood that timing was crucial in the entertainment industry. The rise of social media platforms played a significant role in her journey, allowing her to connect directly with her audience. She frequently engaged with fans on Instagram and Twitter, sharing snippets of her life, behind-the-scenes moments, and her love for music. Her authenticity resonated with fans, fostering a loyal community that celebrated her achievements and supported her every step of the way.

In late 2015, Sabrina released her debut EP, Eyes Wide Open, which featured hits like "All We Have Is Love" and "White Flag." The EP's release showcased her evolution as an artist and further established her presence in the music scene. Each song reflected her personal experiences and growth, revealing the depth of her artistry. The EP received positive reviews, with critics praising her unique sound and heartfelt lyrics.

Sabrina's charm and talent also caught the attention of music industry heavyweights. She collaborated with notable artists, including The Vamps and Jonas Blue, expanding her musical repertoire and reaching wider audiences. These collaborations not only showcased her versatility but also introduced her to new fans who appreciated her distinct sound. Sabrina's ability to seamlessly blend pop, folk, and R&B elements further solidified her reputation as a multifaceted artist.

As her popularity soared, Sabrina found herself balancing her dual career as both an actress and a musician. She starred in various television shows and films while simultaneously working on new music.

The release of her single "Thumbs" in 2016 marked a significant milestone in her career, earning her acclaim for its catchy beat and relatable lyrics. The accompanying music video showcased her playful personality and further endeared her to fans.

Despite the whirlwind of success, Sabrina remained grounded and focused on her artistry. She used her platform to advocate for important causes, including mental health awareness and anti-bullying initiatives. Her genuine commitment to using her voice for positive change resonated with her audience, enhancing her connection with fans who admired her dedication.

Breaking into the spotlight was not just about fame for Sabrina; it was about forging meaningful connections and inspiring others through her music. Her journey was a testament to the power of hard work, resilience, and authenticity in an industry that can often feel overwhelming. With each performance, she shone brighter, leaving audiences eager to see what this talented young star would achieve next.

The Impact of Social Media

In the digital age, social media has become an essential tool for artists to connect with their audiences, and for Sabrina Carpenter, it played a pivotal role in launching her career. As she stepped into the limelight, platforms like YouTube, Instagram, and Twitter provided her with a unique opportunity to showcase her personality, talent, and creativity directly to fans.

Sabrina's journey on social media began with her YouTube channel, where she initially shared covers of popular songs. Her charming videos quickly gained traction, attracting viewers who admired her vocal abilities and relatable demeanor. One of her early covers, a rendition of "Stand By Me," showcased not only her singing talent but also her ability to connect emotionally with her audience. Viewers were drawn to her authenticity and genuine passion for music, leading to a steady increase in subscribers and followers.

As she gained recognition, Sabrina embraced the power of social media to engage with her fans on a personal level. She frequently shared snippets of her life, behind-the-scenes moments from her shows, and even glimpses of her songwriting process.

Whether she was sharing a fun moment with friends or posting a candid selfie, her posts radiated warmth and authenticity, fostering a sense of connection that her fans deeply appreciated.

One memorable instance was when Sabrina hosted a live Q&A session on Instagram, allowing her fans to ask questions about her music, acting, and life in general. This direct interaction created a community where fans felt heard and valued. Sabrina's willingness to share her experiences, both the highs and lows, made her relatable and inspiring to many young people navigating their own journeys.

The visual appeal of her social media presence also contributed to her growing popularity. Her vibrant, colorful posts reflected her cheerful personality and unique sense of style. Sabrina often showcased her fashion choices, collaborating with various brands to create eye-catching outfits that resonated with her audience. This blend of personal style and artistic expression further solidified her status as a fashion icon among her fans.

As her music career blossomed, social media became a powerful platform for promoting her releases.

When she dropped her singles, she would create excitement through countdowns, sneak peeks, and interactive stories. Fans eagerly anticipated new music, feeling like they were part of the journey. Sabrina's dedication to keeping her followers informed and engaged was key in building anticipation for each project.

Moreover, her social media presence allowed her to address important issues and advocate for causes close to her heart. Sabrina frequently used her platform to raise awareness about mental health, self-love, and anti-bullying initiatives. By sharing personal stories and encouraging her followers to embrace their uniqueness, she empowered her fans to be confident and resilient.

The impact of social media on Sabrina Carpenter's career cannot be overstated. It transformed her from a talented actress into a multifaceted artist with a dedicated fanbase. By embracing the digital world, she created a space where her music could thrive and her message could resonate. Through her heartfelt interactions and uplifting content, Sabrina became not just a star but a role model for many, inspiring them to chase their dreams and embrace their true selves.

Chapter 5

- Chart-Topping Hits: Explore the songs that brought her fame and the stories behind them, including fan favorites.
- Fan Reactions: Understand how her music resonated with audiences, leading to a dedicated fanbase.
- Navigating Fame: Learn about the challenges and joys of becoming a star, including balancing public life and personal growth.

The Rise to Stardom

Chart-Topping Hits

As Sabrina Carpenter's career took off, her music began to dominate the airwaves, leading her to create a string of chart-topping hits that showcased her unique artistry and resonated deeply with her fans. Each song told a story, reflecting her personal experiences, relationships, and the journey of growing up in the spotlight.

One of her breakout singles, "Thumbs," released in 2016, marked a significant turning point in her career. This catchy pop anthem, with its infectious chorus and relatable lyrics, quickly climbed the charts and captured the hearts of listeners everywhere. In the song, Sabrina explored themes of independence and self-empowerment, celebrating the strength of individual choices and the importance of staying true to oneself. The vibrant music video, filled with energetic choreography and playful visuals, further solidified its status as a fan favorite.

Sabrina's collaboration with fellow artist Khalid on the song "All We Have Is Love" showcased her ability to blend her style with other musical influences. The track's uplifting message and soulful melodies resonated with fans, emphasizing the significance of love and support in difficult times.

Their chemistry in the music video was palpable, creating a visual narrative that spoke to the heart.

In 2019, Sabrina released "In My Bed," another hit that garnered widespread acclaim. This song, co-written by Sabrina herself, delved into the complexities of relationships and self-reflection. The lyrics poignantly captured the feelings of longing and vulnerability that many young listeners could relate to. The accompanying music video featured vibrant aesthetics and playful imagery, mirroring the upbeat yet introspective nature of the song.

Her ability to weave personal stories into her music extended to the poignant track "Skinny Dipping." In this heartfelt song, Sabrina shared her experiences of vulnerability and self-acceptance. The emotional depth and honesty in the lyrics struck a chord with fans, who praised her for addressing topics that often went unspoken. The track quickly became an anthem for those embracing their true selves, further solidifying Sabrina's place as a relatable figure in the music industry.

As each new release built upon her growing discography, Sabrina continued to explore various musical styles, infusing her songs with elements of pop, R&B, and even hints of folk.

This versatility attracted a diverse audience, allowing her to connect with fans from all walks of life. Her willingness to experiment with different genres kept her sound fresh and exciting, making each release a highly anticipated event.

Behind each chart-topping hit was a story waiting to be told. Sabrina often drew inspiration from her own life experiences, relationships, and the world around her. The lyrics became a canvas for her emotions, allowing her to express thoughts and feelings that resonated with her audience. Whether it was through catchy hooks or heartfelt ballads, she painted vivid pictures of the joys and challenges of growing up.

As her music reached greater heights, Sabrina Carpenter's authenticity and relatability remained at the forefront. Fans resonated with her journey through love, friendship, and self-discovery, making each song an anthem for their own experiences. Her ability to connect on a personal level transformed her hits into soundtracks for the lives of many, solidifying her status as a beloved artist in the hearts of her fans.

Fan Reactions

From the moment "Thumbs" hit the airwaves, fans took to social media to express their admiration. Many shared personal stories of how the song's empowering message helped them through tough times, emphasizing the importance of self-love and individuality. One fan tweeted, "This song makes me feel like I can conquer anything! Thank you, Sabrina!" Such sentiments echoed throughout her fanbase, creating a strong sense of community and shared experience.

Sabrina's music videos became a visual representation of her artistic vision, and fans eagerly awaited their release. The vibrant aesthetics, combined with her engaging performances, often sparked discussions and fan theories online. For instance, the visuals in "In My Bed" were met with praise for their creative storytelling. Fans commented on how they felt an emotional connection to the characters in the video, making them feel seen and understood. One fan remarked, "The way she portrays these feelings is exactly how I feel! It's like she knows me!"

Sabrina's performances, whether at local showcases or larger events, were met with thunderous applause and cheering.

Attendees often described the electrifying atmosphere, with many taking to platforms like Instagram to share clips and photos from her shows. During one memorable performance at a music festival in 2019, fans sang along to every word of her songs, creating an unforgettable experience. The camaraderie among fans was palpable, as they bonded over shared lyrics and favorite moments from her music.

As her popularity soared, Sabrina's interactions with her fans became a cherished aspect of her career. She frequently engaged with them on social media, responding to comments and sharing behind-the-scenes glimpses of her life. This authenticity endeared her even more to her followers, who felt a personal connection with her. Fans would often post heartfelt messages, thanking her for being a positive influence in their lives. One fan shared, "Sabrina's music has been my safe place. Her honesty inspires me every day!"

Sabrina's concerts transformed into joyous celebrations of her music and the strong community she built.

With each performance, fans would create banners and signs, expressing their love and support for her journey. The overwhelming enthusiasm made each event feel like a family reunion, where everyone came together to celebrate not just Sabrina's music but the shared experiences that brought them all together.

The reactions to her music extended beyond just enjoyment; many fans found solace and strength in her lyrics. Songs like "Skinny Dipping" encouraged listeners to embrace their authenticity, fostering a sense of acceptance within her fan community. Her ability to tackle themes of vulnerability and self-acceptance resonated with many, leading to heartfelt conversations among fans. In online forums, fans would discuss their personal journeys, often citing Sabrina's music as a catalyst for their growth.

In an industry where artists often feel distant from their fans, Sabrina Carpenter's genuine interactions and heartfelt music bridged that gap. Her ability to connect through her lyrics and performances created a lasting impact, turning casual listeners into devoted supporters. Each song became more than just a melody; it became a source of inspiration, a reminder that they were all on this journey of life together.

Navigating Fame

One of the first challenges Sabrina faced was the pressure of maintaining her authenticity while navigating the music industry. With her debut album, "Eyes Wide Open," released in 2015, the stakes were high. She reflected on this time in her life, saying, "It was exciting, but I had to learn who I was amidst all the noise." This realization led her to focus on what mattered most: her music and the connection she had with her fans.

The rapid rise to fame often meant public scrutiny. Sabrina quickly learned that not every comment or review would be positive. The key was to stay true to herself, regardless of outside opinions. She shared her thoughts in interviews, stating, "I've learned that you can't please everyone, and that's okay. What matters is that I'm being honest in my art." This mindset allowed her to embrace criticism and transform it into motivation.

The balancing act between personal life and public persona was another aspect of navigating fame. Sabrina found joy in her friendships and family, making it essential to keep her loved ones close. She often credited her parents, David and Elizabeth Carpenter, for their unwavering support. "They remind me of who I am and where I came from," she said, highlighting their role in helping her stay grounded.

Despite the challenges, Sabrina embraced the opportunities that came with her success. She participated in various charity events, using her platform to raise awareness for causes close to her heart, such as mental health and education. These experiences not only enriched her life but also deepened her connection with fans who admired her for her genuine desire to make a difference.

Additionally, she learned to adapt to the rapid pace of the entertainment industry. Touring, recording, and promoting her music often meant long hours and tight schedules. However, Sabrina approached each challenge with determination. "It's tiring, but when I see my fans' faces at concerts, it all makes sense," she shared. This passion for her craft fueled her dedication and allowed her to embrace the chaos of fame.

Sabrina also took the time to reflect on her experiences, often documenting her thoughts in a journal. This practice became a form of self-care, helping her process the ups and downs of her journey. She revealed in a candid moment, "Writing has always been my escape. It helps me find clarity in the madness."

Chapter 6

- Powerful Partnerships: Delve into notable collaborations with other artists, discussing how they came to be.
- Learning from Others: Understand how these partnerships influenced her growth as a musician and artist.
- Creating Magic Together: Explore memorable moments in the studio and on stage, highlighting the chemistry with her collaborators.

Inspiring Collaborations

Powerful Partnerships

Sabrina Carpenter's musical journey has been marked by a series of remarkable collaborations that have enriched her artistry and expanded her reach in the industry. These partnerships didn't just happen by chance; they were a blend of hard work, mutual admiration, and serendipitous moments that brought talented artists together.

One of her early and notable collaborations was with Jonas Blue on the hit single "Perfect," released in 2017. The partnership came about through a shared connection in the music industry, as both artists admired each other's work. Sabrina reminisced about the experience, saying, "I had been a fan of Jonas's music for a while. When the opportunity arose, I was thrilled. It felt like a dream come true!" Their creative synergy was evident as they blended their styles to produce a fresh sound that resonated with fans worldwide.

Another significant collaboration was with Alessia Cara on the empowering anthem "On Purpose." The song, featured on Sabrina's album "Emails I Can't Send," showcases both artists' distinct vocal styles and lyrical prowess.

The collaboration was born out of mutual respect; both Sabrina and Alessia had been inspired by each other's journeys. "When we got in the studio together, it felt like we were meant to create something special," Sabrina shared, emphasizing the natural chemistry they had. The song's theme of self-acceptance struck a chord with many listeners, illustrating how their collaboration extended beyond music into a message of empowerment.

In addition to these noteworthy partnerships, Sabrina also found joy in collaborating with fellow Disney Channel stars, such as Maddie Ziegler and Dove Cameron. Their friendships blossomed into creative alliances, resulting in memorable performances and music videos. Sabrina fondly recalls the fun they had shooting the video for "All We Have Is Love," where they celebrated friendship and the importance of support. "We just had a blast. It felt like a girls' day out mixed with creativity!" she laughed, highlighting how collaboration can be both a professional and personal experience.

These powerful partnerships not only showcased her versatility as an artist but also deepened her appreciation for collaboration in the music industry.

Each experience offered valuable lessons and new perspectives, helping her grow as a musician. "Working with other artists teaches you so much," she explained. "You learn about their process, their style, and it pushes you to be better."

Through these collaborations, Sabrina Carpenter has shown that music is not just about individual talent; it's about the magic that happens when artists come together, bringing their unique voices to the table. Each partnership has left an indelible mark on her career, fueling her passion for creativity and solidifying her place in the ever-evolving landscape of the music industry.

Learning from Others

Sabrina often cites Kesha as one of her inspirations, both musically and personally. When they teamed up for a special performance at a charity event, Sabrina was in awe of Kesha's dynamic presence and unapologetic authenticity. "Kesha taught me about embracing who you are and being fearless in your creativity," she reflects. This collaboration allowed Sabrina to witness firsthand how Kesha used her platform to advocate for self-acceptance and resilience. Sabrina took those lessons to heart, applying them not only in her music but also in how she approached her fans and public persona.

Another pivotal collaboration occurred when she worked with The Vamps on a project that combined their distinct sounds. While in the studio, Sabrina marveled at how they approached songwriting. "Their process was so different from mine," she recalled. "They focused on creating an infectious energy right from the start." This experience taught her the value of spontaneity and embracing the moment in the creative process, something she incorporated into her future projects.

Sabrina's collaboration with Lauv on the song "All We Have Is Love" was another defining moment. Their partnership was built on a mutual understanding of the emotional depths of music. "Lauv and I would talk about our experiences, and it helped shape the song," she explained. The way he expressed vulnerability in his lyrics inspired her to dig deeper into her own songwriting. Through this collaboration, she learned the importance of storytelling and authenticity, which became central to her creative identity.

Every artist she worked with offered a unique lesson, shaping her evolution in the music world. "Each collaboration is like a class in itself," Sabrina shared. "You learn about different genres, rhythms, and ways to connect with listeners. It's all about growth." These experiences have not only enhanced her musical skills but also broadened her perspective on the power of collaboration in art.

Sabrina's journey illustrates the significance of learning from others in the creative process. By embracing the lessons from her collaborators, she has continued to evolve as an artist, crafting a sound that reflects both her individuality and the rich tapestry of influences she has encountered along the way.

Creating Magic Together

In the world of music, some moments are truly magical, and Sabrina Carpenter's collaborations have been filled with such enchanting experiences. From the studio to the stage, the chemistry between Sabrina and her fellow artists has produced unforgettable memories and some of her most beloved songs.

One of the most memorable moments came during the recording of "Skinny Dipping", a track that showcases her playful side. Working with Lauv in the studio, Sabrina recalls the energy they created together: "We were laughing, experimenting with sounds, and just having fun. It felt like we were painting a masterpiece." Their collaborative spirit led to a vibrant, catchy song that resonated with fans, illustrating the power of joy in the creative process.

Another highlight was her collaboration with Tinashe for the track "Bad Time". The two artists decided to experiment with different styles and vibes, blending Tinashe's sultry pop with Sabrina's more upbeat sound. "We were just two girls having a blast, trying out all these cool ideas," Sabrina says. The camaraderie they shared not only made the recording enjoyable but also resulted in a dynamic song that showcases their respective strengths.

On stage, Sabrina's performances with Jonas Blue during live shows were equally captivating. The excitement of performing "Perfect" together brought a spark to their shows that fans loved. "There's nothing like sharing the stage with someone who's just as passionate about the music," she reflects. Their chemistry lit up the audience, creating a memorable experience that fans still talk about.

Additionally, during her tours, Sabrina often invites guest artists to join her for surprise duets. One night, she brought out Jodie Sweetin, her former co-star from Girl Meets World, to sing a few nostalgic tunes. "It was so special to share that moment with her and reminisce about our time together," Sabrina shares. These unexpected collaborations not only delight the audience but also strengthen the bonds of friendship and artistry.

Sabrina Carpenter's journey in music is woven with moments of connection and creativity. Through her collaborations, she not only creates captivating music but also builds lasting friendships. Each song, performance, and studio session is a testament to the magic that happens when artists come together, inspiring one another and their fans.

Chapter 7

- Facing Challenges: Learn about the hurdles Sabrina encountered on her journey, from industry pressures to personal struggles.
- Resilience and Strength: Discover how she found the strength to keep going, even in tough times, and the support she received.
- Lessons Learned: Reflect on the valuable insights gained from tough times and how they shaped her as an artist and person.

Overcoming Obstacles

Facing Challenges

Every star's journey to the top is often sprinkled with obstacles, and Sabrina Carpenter is no exception. Behind the glitz and glamour of her rise to fame lie moments of uncertainty and struggle that have shaped her into the resilient artist she is today.

One of the most significant challenges Sabrina faced was the pressure of the entertainment industry. Starting her career at a young age, she quickly realized that being in the spotlight came with its own set of expectations. "I felt like I was constantly being judged, not just for my music, but for who I was as a person," she admits. The scrutiny was intense, and at times, it took a toll on her mental health. The weight of expectations from fans, critics, and even herself made the journey daunting. "It was hard to find my footing when everything felt so overwhelming," she shares.

Sabrina also encountered personal struggles that added to her challenges. During her early teen years, she experienced the typical ups and downs of adolescence, but with a heightened public awareness.

"Navigating friendships, relationships, and growing up in front of everyone's eyes was tough," she reflects. She often turned to her family and close friends for support during these times, reminding herself that she wasn't alone in her feelings. Her mother, Elizabeth Carpenter, played a crucial role in her life, always encouraging Sabrina to stay true to herself and to seek balance in her hectic schedule.

Another hurdle came during her transition from acting to a full-fledged music career. Many questioned whether she could succeed in both fields. "There were times when people doubted my abilities, especially when I decided to pursue music seriously," she recalls. This skepticism fueled her determination, pushing her to prove that she could excel in multiple areas. With every song she released and every performance she delivered, Sabrina showed the world that she was more than just a talented actress; she was a formidable musician in her own right.

The pressure intensified with the rapid pace of social media, where every misstep could quickly become a trending topic. Sabrina learned to navigate this new landscape with caution, understanding that not all attention was positive.

"I had to develop a thicker skin," she says, realizing that criticism is often just part of the journey. By surrounding herself with supportive people and focusing on her passion, she found a way to rise above negativity.

Despite these challenges, Sabrina's story is one of perseverance. Each hurdle she faced not only tested her strength but also solidified her resolve to keep pursuing her dreams. Through her experiences, she learned the importance of self-care and the power of surrounding herself with a supportive network. These trials ultimately shaped her character, making her a beacon of inspiration for many. "If anything, the obstacles taught me to keep pushing forward, no matter how tough it gets," she concludes, proving that every challenge can be transformed into a stepping stone toward success.

Resilience and Strength

Resilience is a quality that shines brightly in Sabrina Carpenter's journey, and it's one of the key ingredients that has allowed her to navigate the tumultuous waters of fame. Throughout her career, she has faced numerous setbacks and challenges, but each time she has risen stronger, proving that true strength comes from within.

One of the most pivotal moments that showcased her resilience occurred when she faced backlash for her choices, both personal and professional. In the music industry, criticism can often feel personal, and Sabrina experienced her fair share of it. "There were moments when I felt like the whole world was against me," she recalls. Yet, instead of succumbing to negativity, she chose to lean into her passion for music as a source of healing. Writing became her refuge. "Whenever I felt overwhelmed, I would write. It was like therapy," she shares, highlighting how songwriting allowed her to channel her feelings and find clarity amidst chaos.

Support from her family, particularly her close-knit group, was crucial during these trying times. Sabrina's parents, David and Elizabeth Carpenter, instilled in her the importance of resilience from a young age. They encouraged her to embrace challenges as opportunities for growth. "They taught me that it's okay to stumble, as long as you get back up," she reflects. This mindset not only helped her persevere through tough moments but also inspired her to be a source of strength for others.

Through her journey, Sabrina has also found inspiration in the stories of other artists who have overcome adversity. "Listening to their experiences made me realize that I wasn't alone in my struggles," she explains. Drawing strength from the journeys of those who came before her, she learned that resilience is not just about enduring hardships but also about rising with grace and courage.

Sabrina's resilience has been beautifully reflected in her music. Songs like "Skinny Dipping" reveal her ability to transform pain into powerful melodies. "Writing those songs was cathartic for me," she notes.

Through her lyrics, she not only expresses her emotions but also offers a sense of connection to her listeners, showing them that it's okay to feel vulnerable.

Her experiences have also taught her the value of self-love and acceptance. "I learned to embrace every part of myself, flaws and all," she says. This realization allowed her to approach her career with a newfound confidence, knowing that she was worthy of love and success, no matter what challenges lay ahead.

In the face of adversity, Sabrina Carpenter stands as a testament to the power of resilience and strength. Her journey is a reminder that while obstacles may arise, the determination to overcome them can lead to personal growth and fulfillment. "Every challenge has shaped me into the artist I am today," she concludes, inspiring countless fans to embrace their own struggles with the same tenacity.

Lessons Learned

Every twist and turn on Sabrina Carpenter's journey has imparted invaluable lessons that have shaped her into the artist and individual she is today. Through her experiences—both the joyful milestones and the challenging obstacles—she has gained insights that resonate deeply with her fans and followers.

One of the most significant lessons Sabrina learned is the importance of authenticity. Early in her career, she faced pressure to conform to industry standards, often feeling as though she had to fit into a specific mold to be successful. However, with time, she recognized that her uniqueness was her greatest strength. "I realized that it's okay to be different," she shares. "Embracing who I am has opened so many doors for me." This revelation not only influenced her music but also empowered her to encourage her fans to be true to themselves.

Sabrina's journey has also taught her the value of perseverance. During moments of doubt, she often recalled the times she had faced challenges and emerged victorious. "Every setback is a setup for a comeback," she reflects, a mantra she adopted to keep herself motivated.

This perspective helped her navigate the uncertainties of the music industry, reminding her that every obstacle was an opportunity to learn and grow.

Moreover, she has learned that vulnerability is a strength, not a weakness. Sharing her struggles through her music has created a deeper connection with her audience. Songs like "All We Have Is Love" illustrate this beautifully, as they speak to the power of love and support during tough times. "When I share my experiences, it not only helps me heal but also lets others know they're not alone," she explains. By opening up about her vulnerabilities, Sabrina fosters a sense of community among her listeners, proving that it's okay to express emotions and seek help.

Sabrina also emphasizes the importance of surrounding oneself with a supportive network. Her close relationships with family, friends, and fellow artists have been crucial in helping her navigate the highs and lows of her career. "Having people who genuinely care about you makes a world of difference," she says. She credits her parents, David and Elizabeth, for their unwavering support and guidance, often reflecting on the family values they instilled in her.

. Their encouragement to pursue her dreams has been a guiding light throughout her journey.

Lastly, Sabrina's journey has reinforced the idea that success is not solely defined by fame or recognition but by personal fulfillment and happiness. "I've learned that what truly matters is doing what you love and making a positive impact," she asserts. This philosophy drives her to create music that resonates with her heart, rather than merely chasing trends. Her focus on authenticity and passion has not only enriched her career but has also inspired countless fans to pursue their dreams with courage and conviction.

In the end, Sabrina Carpenter's journey is not just a tale of stardom but a collection of lessons that encourage resilience, authenticity, and the pursuit of one's passions. Through her music and her story, she reminds us all that while the path may be winding, every experience is a stepping stone toward becoming the best version of ourselves.

Chapter 8

- Awards and Recognition: Relive the accolades and honors she has received, including nominations and wins.
- Milestones in Her Career: Highlight key moments that define her success, including album releases and major tours.
- Giving Back: Explore her philanthropic efforts and contributions to various causes that are close to her heart.

Celebrating Achievements

Awards and Recognition

Sabrina Carpenter's career has been a tapestry woven with accolades and honors, showcasing her talent and hard work. As she made her mark in the entertainment industry, her achievements began to stack up, each one representing a significant milestone in her journey.

One of the earliest recognitions came in 2016 when she received her first nomination for a Teen Choice Award for "Choice TV Actress" for her role in the popular Disney Channel series "Girl Meets World." This nomination was a testament to her talent and the connection she had forged with her audience at such a young age. While she didn't win that year, it was the start of a series of nominations that would soon follow.

In 2017, Sabrina's music career took off, leading to her nomination for iHeartRadio Music Awards in the "Best New Pop Artist" category. The excitement surrounding this nomination was palpable, as fans rallied behind her, showing their support through social media and online votes. It was a proud moment for Sabrina, who shared, "To be recognized by such a significant platform felt surreal. It made me realize that I was truly on the right path."

Sabrina's first major award win came in 2019 when she was honored with the Kids' Choice Award for "Favorite Female Voice from an Animated Movie" for her work in the animated film "The Lion Guard." This accolade was particularly special to her, as it highlighted her versatility as both an actress and a musician. "Winning that award meant the world to me," she recalled. "It was a reflection of my hard work and the love of my fans."

Over the years, she continued to accumulate accolades, including nominations for People's Choice Awards and MTV Movie & TV Awards. Each nomination and win filled her with gratitude and determination to keep pushing her creative boundaries. "Every time I get recognized, it drives me to be better and to create music that resonates with people," Sabrina stated passionately.

In 2021, Sabrina received the Hollywood Music in Media Award for her song "Skinny Dipping," further establishing her presence in the music scene. This recognition not only celebrated her songwriting skills but also showcased her growth as an artist. Sabrina expressed her excitement, saying, "It's incredible to see the fruits of your labor being acknowledged, especially in such a competitive industry."

Beyond individual accolades, Sabrina has also been a part of various projects that have received critical acclaim. For instance, her role in the Netflix film "Tall Girl" showcased her acting chops and garnered positive reviews, solidifying her status as a multi-talented performer. The film's success led to a sequel, demonstrating the impact of her contributions to the project.

As she continues to grow and evolve as an artist, Sabrina Carpenter's awards and recognitions serve as milestones in her career, highlighting the dedication, passion, and talent that she brings to every project. With each honor, she remains focused on her craft, using these achievements as stepping stones toward even greater heights. "I'm just getting started," she reminds her fans with a bright smile. "There's so much more I want to do, and I can't wait to share it all with you."

Milestones in Her Career

One of the first pivotal moments in her career came with the debut of "Girl Meets World" in 2014, a spin-off of the beloved show "Boy Meets World." In this series, Sabrina played the character Maya Hart, which not only showcased her acting talent but also her ability to connect with a younger audience. The show ran for three seasons, allowing her to gain invaluable experience and establish a strong fanbase.

As the series gained popularity, Sabrina also explored her musical aspirations. In 2015, she released her first EP titled "Can't Blame a Girl for Trying." This project featured songs that highlighted her storytelling abilities and showcased her distinct voice. The title track resonated with many young listeners, and its success marked a significant step in her music career. This was followed by her first full-length album, "Eyes Wide Open," in 2017, which debuted to critical acclaim and solidified her presence in the music industry.

The release of her album led to Sabrina embarking on her first concert tour, "The De-Tour," in 2018. This tour allowed her to connect with fans in a more intimate setting and share her music with audiences across the country.

The thrill of performing on stage for her supporters was a dream come true, and she embraced every moment. "The energy from the crowd is something I can't explain. It fuels me," she shared during an interview.

Another major milestone came in 2020 when Sabrina starred in the Netflix film "Tall Girl." The film became a massive hit, and her portrayal of the lead character, Jodi, resonated with viewers, particularly young girls navigating the challenges of self-acceptance and confidence. The success of "Tall Girl" opened doors for Sabrina in the film industry, leading to her involvement in various other projects, including the sequel, which was released in 2022.

In 2021, Sabrina reached another significant milestone with the release of her highly anticipated album, "Emails I Can't Send." The album showcased her growth as a songwriter and artist, with deeply personal lyrics that resonated with listeners. Songs like "Skinny Dipping" and "Vicious" highlighted her evolution, both musically and emotionally. The album's success demonstrated her ability to tackle complex themes and connect with fans on a deeper level.

Giving Back

One of the causes that Sabrina is particularly passionate about is mental health awareness. She has spoken openly about the importance of mental health and has encouraged her fans to seek help and support when they need it. In 2019, she participated in a campaign for Mental Health Awareness Month, where she shared her own experiences and emphasized the significance of self-care and breaking the stigma surrounding mental health issues. "It's okay not to be okay," she shared in a heartfelt message to her followers, reminding them that reaching out for help is a sign of strength.

Sabrina has also been actively involved in charitable initiatives. In 2020, she collaborated with the organization No Kid Hungry, which works to end childhood hunger in America. As part of this partnership, she participated in fundraising events and used her social media platforms to raise awareness about the issue. "Every child deserves access to healthy food," she expressed passionately during a charity livestream. Her dedication to this cause has helped shine a light on the importance of fighting hunger and supporting families in need.

Another area close to Sabrina's heart is environmental sustainability. She has often advocated for eco-friendly practices and has encouraged her fans to be mindful of their environmental impact. In 2021, she took part in a campaign to promote Earth Day, where she shared tips on how to live a more sustainable lifestyle, from reducing waste to supporting eco-conscious brands. "We all have a responsibility to protect our planet," she stated, inspiring her fans to take action in their own lives.

In addition to these causes, Sabrina has also been involved in various projects supporting education. She has partnered with organizations that provide scholarships and resources to underprivileged youth, emphasizing the importance of education in shaping futures. Through her efforts, she hopes to empower young people to pursue their dreams and achieve their goals.

Sabrina Carpenter's philanthropic work reflects her genuine desire to make a positive impact in the world. Her advocacy for mental health, commitment to ending childhood hunger, dedication to environmental sustainability, and support for education showcase her compassionate spirit.

Chapter 9

- Her Unique Style: Discover Sabrina's fashion choices and signature looks, including her favorite designers and trends.
- Favorite Things: Learn about her hobbies, interests, and inspirations outside of music, including books, movies, and food.
- Building Connections: Understand how she engages with her fans through social media, meet-and-greets, and special events.

Fashion, Favorites, and Fan Bonds

Her Unique Style

Sabrina Carpenter's fashion journey is as vibrant and dynamic as her music career. With her keen sense of style, she has become a role model for many young fans, showcasing a unique blend of elegance, fun, and individuality that shines through in her outfits. Each appearance she makes, whether on the red carpet or at casual outings, tells a story of creativity and self-expression.

From an early age, Sabrina displayed an interest in fashion. Growing up in Lehigh Valley, Pennsylvania, she often experimented with her wardrobe, inspired by her family and friends. She has fond memories of rummaging through her older sister's closet, trying on different outfits, and discovering her own sense of style. "Fashion is like art to me," she once remarked, emphasizing how it allows her to express her personality without saying a word.

One of Sabrina's favorite designers is Christian Siriano, known for his stunning, whimsical designs. She has been seen wearing his creations at various events, including the 2017 Teen Choice Awards, where she wowed in a striking floral gown that perfectly complemented her radiant personality. Another designer she adores is Marc Jacobs, whose playful yet sophisticated styles resonate with her.

At the 2021 Kids' Choice Awards, she sported a chic ensemble featuring bold colors and patterns, making a fashion statement that turned heads.

Sabrina is also known for her love of streetwear, often mixing high-fashion pieces with casual attire. For instance, she's frequently spotted in oversized hoodies paired with stylish combat boots, creating a relaxed yet fashionable look. In her everyday life, she enjoys wearing comfortable yet trendy outfits that reflect her youthful spirit, such as graphic tees with vintage jeans or cute sundresses adorned with playful prints.

Accessorizing is another aspect of her style that she loves to explore. Sabrina has a penchant for statement jewelry, particularly oversized earrings and layered necklaces that add flair to her outfits. One memorable moment was at a Los Angeles premiere in 2018, where she donned an eye-catching pair of iridescent hoops that perfectly complemented her vibrant look. She often emphasizes that the right accessories can elevate any outfit, making it feel fresh and exciting.

Sabrina's influence in fashion is not just about her choices but also how she embraces her personal journey. She often encourages her fans to express themselves through their clothing, inspiring them to be confident in their skin.

"Your style is a reflection of who you are. Own it!" she has said, fostering a sense of empowerment among her followers.

With her keen eye for fashion and an ever-evolving wardrobe, Sabrina Carpenter continues to inspire many with her unique style, showcasing the importance of self-expression and creativity in all aspects of life.

Favorite Things

Sabrina Carpenter's personality is a vibrant tapestry woven from her many favorite things— hobbies, interests, and inspirations that shape her life and connect her deeply with her fans. Each element adds depth and relatability to her character, creating a bond with those who admire her.

One of Sabrina's cherished interests is literature. She has a profound love for storytelling and often immerses herself in books that transport her to different worlds. Among her favorite authors is Sarah Dessen, whose novels explore themes of love, friendship, and self-discovery. Sabrina is particularly fond of Dessen's "Just Listen," which she cites as a significant influence on her understanding of emotions and relationships. She often shares her reading lists with fans, encouraging them to dive into the literary adventures that have inspired her.

Movies hold a special place in Sabrina's heart, too. She enjoys a wide array of films, from animated classics to contemporary dramas. A standout favorite is "The Princess Diaries," a tale that resonates with her own journey in the entertainment industry.

The themes of self-discovery and finding one's voice mirror her experiences. She loves hosting movie nights with friends, where they indulge in feel-good films that uplift their spirits. Her taste also includes romantic comedies like "Crazy, Stupid, Love" and powerful dramas like "A Star Is Born."

Music is, of course, another passion for Sabrina. Her eclectic taste spans various genres, including pop, folk, R&B, and alternative rock. She admires artists such as Taylor Swift, whose storytelling ability in songwriting inspires her creativity. Sabrina has expressed her appreciation for Adele's emotive performances, often sharing snippets of their songs on social media, encouraging fans to embrace the raw emotions in music. Her playlists are a reflection of her current mood, featuring tracks that inspire, uplift, or provide comfort.

Food also plays a significant role in Sabrina's life. She has a particular fondness for comfort foods, and her go-to favorites include macaroni and cheese, chocolate chip cookies, and pizza— especially when shared with friends during cozy get-togethers. She fondly remembers baking with her mom during her childhood, creating sweet memories in the kitchen filled with the aromas of freshly baked treats.

Sabrina loves visiting a local café called Café Bizou, where she enjoys indulging in crepes and mocha lattes, a favorite combination that has become a delightful tradition.

In addition to food, Sabrina has a soft spot for animals, particularly dogs. She is often seen sharing adorable photos of her pet dog, a lovable miniature poodle named Bubbles. The bond they share is evident, and Sabrina frequently mentions how Bubbles brings joy and comfort to her life, especially during busy days. She believes that pets have a unique way of providing unconditional love and support.

Sabrina is also passionate about the outdoors and enjoys spending her free time exploring nature. She often shares her hiking adventures on social media, encouraging her fans to connect with the beauty of the world around them. One of her favorite hiking spots is Runyon Canyon in Los Angeles, where she appreciates the stunning views and the chance to recharge. Nature walks are her way of finding peace amidst her hectic schedule, and she often takes moments to reflect on her experiences and inspirations.

Art is another significant part of Sabrina's life. She enjoys painting and drawing as a form of self-expression.

These creative outlets allow her to explore her artistic side beyond music. She often shares her artwork on her social media, inviting fans to see her journey as an artist in different mediums. Sabrina's passion for art reflects her belief that creativity comes in many forms and encourages her fans to explore their artistic inclinations.

Travel is an adventure that Sabrina cherishes. She has a desire to explore new places and cultures, often sharing her travel experiences with her audience. One of her favorite destinations is Italy, where she fell in love with the rich history, stunning architecture, and delicious cuisine. Sabrina has expressed her dream of visiting all the iconic landmarks, particularly the Colosseum in Rome and the beautiful Amalfi Coast. Her travels inspire her creativity and provide fresh perspectives that often find their way into her music and artistry.

Sabrina Carpenter's favorite things go beyond simple preferences; they create a beautiful narrative that reflects her multifaceted personality. Each book she reads, movie she watches, meal she enjoys, and adventure she undertakes adds a layer of richness to her life.

Building Connections

Sabrina Carpenter understands the power of connection, especially in a world where social media bridges the gap between stars and their fans. Her engagement with followers is a testament to her appreciation for the people who support her journey. Through various platforms, she shares glimpses of her life, music, and inspirations, fostering a sense of community that resonates with her audience.

One of the primary ways Sabrina connects with her fans is through social media. Her platforms, including Instagram, Twitter, and TikTok, serve as virtual spaces where she shares everything from behind-the-scenes looks at her projects to everyday moments that reflect her personality. She often posts candid photos and fun videos, inviting fans into her world. For instance, she has a habit of hosting Q&A sessions on Instagram Live, where she answers questions directly from her followers, making each interaction feel personal and meaningful. This openness allows her fans to feel like they truly know her, deepening their connection.

Meet-and-greet events are another way Sabrina creates lasting bonds with her supporters.

She frequently organizes these gatherings during her tours, offering fans a chance to meet her in person. During these events, she takes the time to listen to their stories and share a few moments together. Sabrina believes that these interactions are special, as they allow her to express her gratitude for their unwavering support. Many fans have shared heartwarming stories about how these moments have impacted their lives, leaving them with cherished memories.

Sabrina also engages in philanthropic efforts, aligning her passions with causes close to her heart. She has been involved in various charity initiatives, including campaigns that support mental health awareness, education, and animal welfare. For instance, she collaborated with organizations like DoSomething.org to encourage young people to take action in their communities. Her dedication to giving back resonates with her fans, who admire her commitment to making a positive impact in the world. Through her charitable work, she shows that her heart extends beyond the stage, inspiring her followers to get involved and support meaningful causes.

Another memorable aspect of her connection with fans comes through her music.

Sabrina's songs often explore themes of love, self-acceptance, and personal growth, allowing her listeners to relate to her experiences. She encourages her fans to share their interpretations of her songs, creating a dialogue that enriches the connection between artist and audience. Fans often express how her lyrics resonate with their own struggles and triumphs, making her music a source of comfort and empowerment.

Special events, such as album release parties and virtual concerts, further solidify her bond with her fans. During these events, she engages in fun activities, such as trivia games and live performances, allowing fans to share in the excitement of new music together. The sense of community at these gatherings is palpable, with fans coming together to celebrate not just her achievements, but their shared love for her artistry. Through her genuine efforts to connect with her audience, Sabrina Carpenter has cultivated a loyal and passionate fanbase. Her ability to share her life authentically, combined with her dedication to uplifting others, creates a warm atmosphere where fans feel seen and valued.

Chapter 10

- Journaling Ideas: Reflect on your own dreams and inspirations, with prompts that encourage personal expression.
- Fun Quizzes: Challenge your knowledge about Sabrina's life and interests with interactive quizzes.

Fun Reflections

Fun Quizzes

- What is Sabrina Carpenter's full name?
- In which year was Sabrina Carpenter born?
- What was Sabrina's breakthrough role on Disney Channel?
- Which song marked her debut in the music industry?
- What are some genres of music that Sabrina explores?
- Which movie did Sabrina star in alongside Sofia Wylie?
- What notable series did she voice a character in?
- Who are some of Sabrina's musical influences?
- What is one of Sabrina's favorite hobbies outside of music?
- Which social media platform does she use most frequently to connect with fans?
- How many siblings does Sabrina have?
- What was the title of her first album?
- Which song from her second album became a hit?
- What is a notable philanthropic effort Sabrina supports?
- What year did Sabrina release her album Emails I Can't Send?

- What is the name of her character in Girl Meets World?
- Which fashion designer is Sabrina known to favor?
- What is a recurring theme in Sabrina's music?
- In what year did she start her YouTube channel?
- Which famous song did she cover that received widespread praise?
- What is the title of Sabrina's collaboration with Alan Walker?
- What inspired her song "Skinny Dipping"?
- What was a significant milestone in her career in 2021?
- What is a favorite pastime for Sabrina when she has free time?
- How does Sabrina engage with her fans during her tours?
- What kind of pets does Sabrina have?
- What kind of roles does Sabrina express interest in pursuing?
- What was one of Sabrina's childhood aspirations?
- What is a unique aspect of Sabrina's concerts?
- What does Sabrina advocate for through her platform?

Answers

- Sabrina Anne Carpenter.
- She was born on May 11, 1999.
- She gained fame for her role as Maya Hart on the series Girl Meets World.
- Sabrina released her debut single, "Can't Blame a Girl for Trying," in 2013.
- Her music spans various genres, including pop, folk, and R&B.
- She starred in the Disney Channel original movie Tall Girl in 2019.
- Sabrina voiced the character "Ava" in the animated series Tangled: The Series.
- She has cited artists like Taylor Swift and Ed Sheeran as inspirations.
- Sabrina loves painting and often shares her artwork with her fans.
- She is very active on Instagram, sharing insights into her life and career.
- Sabrina has two older sisters: Sarah and Shannon.
- Her debut album is titled Eyes Wide Open, released in 2015.
- "Thumbs," from her album Evolution (2016), received significant acclaim.
- She has been involved with various initiatives, including those focused on mental health awareness.

- She released this album in 2022.
- She plays Maya Hart, a talented and spirited teen.
- She has expressed her love for designers like Carolina Herrera and Gucci.
- Many of her songs focus on themes of self-acceptance and personal growth.
- She started her YouTube channel in 2011, sharing music and personal vlogs.
- Sabrina covered "Shout Out to My Ex" by Little Mix, showcasing her vocal talent.
- She collaborated with him on the song "On My Way," released in 2019.
- The song is about embracing one's true self and enjoying life without worry.
- She made her Broadway debut in The Last Five Years.
- She enjoys reading and often shares her favorite books with fans.
- She often holds meet-and-greet events where she interacts with her fans personally.
- She has a dog named Winston, who she adores and often features on her social media.
- She is interested in diverse roles, including those in musicals and dramatic films.

- She dreamed of being an artist and often performed in school plays.
- She often includes interactive elements, encouraging fan participation.
- She actively promotes mental health awareness and encourages her fans to seek help when needed.

journaling prompts

Journaling is a wonderful way to reflect on your thoughts, emotions, and experiences, allowing you to explore your dreams and inspirations in a safe and creative space. Inspired by the journey of Sabrina Carpenter, these prompts encourage you to dive deep into your personal stories, aspirations, and feelings. Whether you're looking to celebrate achievements, navigate challenges, or simply express yourself, these prompts serve as a guiding light for your self-discovery. Grab your favorite notebook or journal, find a cozy spot, and let your imagination flow as you respond to these thoughtful questions. Happy journaling!

- Dream Big: Write about a dream or goal you have for the future. What steps can you take to achieve it?
- Inspiration Station: Who inspires you the most in your life? Write about a specific moment when they influenced you or taught you something valuable.
- Your Soundtrack: Create a playlist of songs that represent your life right now. Explain why each song resonates with you.
- Overcoming Obstacles: Think about a challenge you've faced recently. How did you overcome it, and what did you learn from the experience?
- Moments of Joy: Describe a moment that brought you immense happiness. What made it special, and how can you recreate that feeling?
- Creative Expression: Write a short poem or song lyric about your current emotions. Don't worry about it being perfect; let your creativity flow!
- Friendship Reflections: Think about your closest friends. Write about a fun memory you have together and what makes your friendship special.
- Favorite Things: List your top five favorite things in life. Describe why each one is important to you.

- Looking Up: Write a letter to your future self. What do you hope to have accomplished by then, and what advice would you give yourself?
- Self-Discovery: What are three qualities you love about yourself? How do these qualities help you navigate through life?
- Lessons Learned: Reflect on a mistake you've made and the lesson it taught you. How has that shaped who you are today?
- Daily Gratitude: Write down three things you are grateful for today. How do they contribute to your happiness?
- Your Passion Project: If you could start a project based on something you love, what would it be? Describe it and how you would get started.
- Moments of Courage: Write about a time when you stepped out of your comfort zone. How did it feel, and what did you learn?
- A Letter to Your Role Model: Write a letter to someone you look up to, expressing what you admire about them and how they have impacted your life.
- Future Aspirations: Where do you see yourself in five years? What do you hope to be doing, and how can you start working toward that vision today?

- Coping Strategies: List your favorite ways to cope with stress. Which ones do you find the most effective, and why?
- Creative Space: Describe your ideal creative space. What would it look like, and how would it inspire you?
- Travel Dreams: If you could visit any place in the world, where would it be? Write about what draws you to that location and what you would like to do there.
- Celebrating Achievements: Reflect on a recent accomplishment, big or small. How did it feel to achieve that goal, and what motivated you to succeed?

Fun facts

- A Hidden Talent for Art
- Sabrina has a knack for painting and drawing. When she's not working on music or acting, she often unwinds by creating sketches and experimenting with watercolors.
- Personal Connection to Paris
- Sabrina loves Paris not only for its beauty and culture but also because her family has a tradition of visiting the city. It's one of her favorite travel destinations, and she even takes inspiration from French fashion and style.
- The Kitchen is Her Happy Place
- Besides singing, Sabrina loves baking, especially desserts! She once mentioned that baking cookies is her go-to stress reliever, and she has a soft spot for experimenting with new recipes in the kitchen.
- Self-Taught Guitar Skills
- Sabrina taught herself to play the guitar during her early teen years, primarily by watching YouTube tutorials and practicing with friends. This became a big part of her songwriting process.

- Inspiration from Classic Films
- Sabrina is a fan of classic Hollywood films from the 1950s and 60s. This vintage influence sometimes sneaks into her style and music videos, adding a nostalgic touch to her work.
- Dedicated Family Time
- Family is everything to Sabrina, and despite her busy schedule, she makes it a priority to spend time with them. She even has a family group chat to stay connected while traveling.
- Bookworm at Heart
- Sabrina loves reading, especially mystery novels and poetry. She's mentioned that diving into a good book helps her escape the pressures of the industry, and she even gets ideas for lyrics from her favorite reads.
- Supports Up-and-Coming Artists
- Sabrina is known for her encouragement of new artists and frequently listens to indie musicians for inspiration. She's even shouted out lesser-known artists in interviews to help them gain a following.
- Fear of Heights
- Despite her confidence on stage, Sabrina has a real fear of heights! She still faces it head-on whenever she has to perform at a high-up venue or in any elevated setting.

- Inspiration from Classic Films
- Sabrina is a fan of classic Hollywood films from the 1950s and 60s. This vintage influence sometimes sneaks into her style and music videos, adding a nostalgic touch to her work.
- Dedicated Family Time
- Family is everything to Sabrina, and despite her busy schedule, she makes it a priority to spend time with them. She even has a family group chat to stay connected while traveling.
- Bookworm at Heart
- Sabrina loves reading, especially mystery novels and poetry. She's mentioned that diving into a good book helps her escape the pressures of the industry, and she even gets ideas for lyrics from her favorite reads.
- Supports Up-and-Coming Artists
- Sabrina is known for her encouragement of new artists and frequently listens to indie musicians for inspiration. She's even shouted out lesser-known artists in interviews to help them gain a following.
- Fear of Heights
- Despite her confidence on stage, Sabrina has a real fear of heights! She still faces it head-on whenever she has to perform at a high-up venue or in any elevated setting.

Printed in Great Britain
by Amazon

50780080R00059